A Poetic Look at the

Sermon on the Mount

And Other Sayings from the Synoptic Gospels

Joe Brand

This book is dedicated to my mother, Mildred, who shares my enjoyment of reading and quoting rhyming poetry. I have yet to meet another person who comes closer to living by the Sermon on the Mount than she.

Contents

Acknowledgements

The poet, Dr. Robert Lynn, deserves credit for motivating and encouraging me to develop my hobby of poetry. Several friends and relatives made significant contributions in pointing out grammatical errors, as well theological misunderstandings and problems with iambic wording. I especially thank Thomas Pabst and my sister Vi Whittington for the many hours they spent carefully sorting through all the details with excellent editing suggestions for the manuscript. Credit also goes to my brother, Bill Brand, for some great editing and encouragement. Similarly, Ellen Deem and Vivian Rodriguez provided both encouragement and valuable comments adding significantly to this book. Other siblings, Orlie Brand and Cathy Beere provided insight and encouragement. Dr. Mary Slater deserves credit for introducing me to the poetic concept of Haiku (used in a few of my poems). Sandy Hokanson and Jill Jennings of the Johns Creek Poetry Group provided valuable insight. A special thanks goes to my son and artist, Tom, who created the cover design. Of course, the one who deserves the most credit is our Lord and Savior, Jesus Christ, whose sayings were the basis for this entire book.

Introduction

The poems that follow are based on various sayings of Christ found in the Synoptic Gospels (Matthew, Mark, and Luke). Some are consistent with traditional theological ideas, whereas others may deviate. Still others may seem to question biblical passages or leave the reader with an open question to contemplate. The scriptural passages are presented on the left pages, and each corresponding poem is generally on the facing right page. The exception is when the poem is too long to fit on one page; in this case it starts on the same page as the scriptural passage, so that in all cases, the poem can be read and the biblical reference viewed without flipping a page.

The first chapter covers *The Sermon on the Mount* (Matthew 5, 6, and 7). The second covers *The Sermon on the Plain* (Luke 6:17-49), and the third consists of other sayings of Christ found in the Synoptic Gospels. Although somewhat redundant to include both *The Sermon on the Mount* and *The Sermon on the Plain*, in the latter, a different or sometimes more abbreviated approach is taken on redundant materials.

In a few of the poems, a reference to one of the Ten Commandments is included. In all cases, the numerical reference is consistent with both the Jewish and the

Protestant definition of the Ten Commandments. The Catholic numbering is slightly different.

The primary source for biblical quotations is the New Revised Standard Version [NRSV]. Other sources are the New International Version [NIV], and the King James Version [KJV]. Quotations of Jesus are printed in bold face.

The first poem of Chapter 1 is based on the Beatitudes in the *Sermon on the Mount*. This is an example where I differ from many interpretations. I assume the expression "poor in spirit" means "spiritually poor;" i.e., one who lacks spirituality, an unreligious person, or one with very little faith.

The first two poems of Chapter 2 relate to Luke's version of the Beatitudes. The first introduces the Beatitudes; rather than the scriptural passage appearing on the facing page, verses by William Blake are presented. Blake's poem, in some sense, reflects the Beatitudes in Luke. The following two pages present the scriptural passage and a more detailed poem reflecting the Beatitudes in Luke. The first beatitude in Luke, "Blessed are you who are poor," is similar to the first in Matthew, "Blessed are the poor in spirit." The two groups toward whom Jesus was most hostile were the very religious and the very rich. Thus, it makes sense that the opposite of these groups would be the ones mentioned first as blessed.

Chapter 1

The Sermon on the Mount

Matthew 5:1-12

When Jesus saw the crowds, he went up the mountain; and after he sat down, his disciples came to him. Then he began to speak, and taught them, saying:

"Blessed are the poor in spirit, for theirs is the kingdom of heaven.

"Blessed are those who mourn, for they will be comforted.

"Blessed are the meek, for they will inherit the earth.

"Blessed are those who hunger and thirst for righteousness, for they will be filled.

"Blessed are the merciful, for they will receive mercy.

"Blessed are the pure in heart, for they will see God.

"Blessed are the peacemakers, for they will be called children of God.

"Blessed are those who are persecuted for righteousness' sake, for theirs is the kingdom of heaven.

"Blessed are you when people revile you and persecute you and utter all kinds of evil against you falsely on my account. Rejoice and be glad for your reward is great in heaven, for the same way they persecuted the prophets who were before you. [NRSV]

The Beatitude Attitude

Christ's Speech starts with Beatitudes;
They ought to be great attitudes.
Is there a problem with the first?
Blest is the one whose faith is worst.

"Poor in spirit" means weak faith base,
But could it be that's no disgrace?
What it means makes some folks stumble,
So they claim that it means humble,

If Jesus didn't mean what He said,
Then He'd say something else instead.
He says God's Kingdom is for all,
Even for those whose faith did fall.

Consider one whose faith is strong;
It seems that he can do no wrong.
A peacemaker's a good example;
His many friends seem to be ample.

But he may not have real close friends
Since others' values aren't his end.
He sees both sides of a conflict;
This likely causes friends to kick.

So whether you are gay or sad,
Put trust in Christ and you'll be glad.
If Spiritual state is worst or best,
Just Join God's Kingdom; you'll be blest.

Matthew 5:13-16

"You are the salt of the earth; but if salt has lost its taste, how can its saltiness be restored? It is no longer good for anything, but is thrown out and trampled under foot.

"You are the light of the world. A city built on a hill cannot be hid. No one after lighting a light puts it under the bushel basket, but on the lamp-stand, and it gives light to all in the house. In the same way, let your light shine before others, so that they may see your good works and give glory to your Father in heaven. [NRSV]

(See also Luke 14:34-35)

We're Like Salt & Light

Without much salt your food tastes flat;
And more significant than that,
Devoid of salt, the floor you'd splat.

But too much salt, you'd pass food by;
Blood pressure can be made too high,
And this can cause some folks to die.

Sunlight gives us Vitamin D;
It also helps all people see,
And it's required for a tree.

Too much sun is not the answer
Since it may result in cancer;
Or you'll look old while still a dancer.

And we can make some folks rejoice
As often as they hear our voice
Due to our conversation choice.

Or we may seem overbearing
With our narrow views all airing;
Folks may then depart not caring.

Matthew 5:17-19

"Do not think that I have come to abolish the law or the prophets; I have come not to abolish but to fulfill. For truly I tell you, until heaven and earth pass away, not one letter, not one stroke of a letter, will pass from the law until all is accomplished. Therefore, whoever breaks one of the least of these commandments, and teaches others to do the same, will be called least in the kingdom of heaven; but whoever does them and teaches them will be called great in the kingdom of heaven. [NRSV]

(See also Luke 16:17)

Law Not Destroyed but Fulfilled

Farmers planting hayfields blend in various kinds of seed;*
To obtain a mule, a horse and donkey are made to breed.*
We wear clothing with mixed fibers* to satisfy our needs.
Some men shave entire beards which clearly mars the edges;**
Some shave their entire heads, while others look like hedges.
To approach the holy altar, we invite all to come,
Of every nationality, wherever they are from. ***

Suppose some laws were added to appease the silly day;
And then if one broke any he would surely have to pay.
But now we can ignore some and still be thought okay.
Perhaps the 10 Commandments were what Jesus had in mind,
For they were all repeated in the prophets' books we find.
God in front of Moses carved them in a mountainous park;
They were kept for many centuries in the covenant ark.

* *Leviticus 19:19—You shall keep my statutes. You shall not let your animals breed with a different kind; you shall not sow your field with two kinds of seed; nor shall you put on a garment made of two different materials.* [NRSV]

** *Leviticus 19:27—You shall not round off the hair on your temples or mar the edges of your beard.* [NRSV]

*** *Leviticus 21:17-23, 23:3a—No one of your offspring throughout their generations who has a blemish may approach to offer the food of his God. For no one who has a blemish shall draw near, one who is blind or lame, or one who has a mutilated face or limb too long, or one who has a broken foot or a broken hand, or a hunchback, or a dwarf, or a man with a blemish in his eyes or an itching disease or scabs or crushed testicles.*
   No Ammonite or Moabite shall be admitted to the assembly of the LORD. [NRSV]

Matthew 5:20

For I tell you, unless your righteousness exceeds that of the scribes and Pharisees, you will never enter the kingdom of heaven. [NRSV]

Righteousness of Scribes and Pharisees

Scribes knew the law in minutest detail;
They'd work to teach and keep the law as well.
Not commit adultery nor take a life,
Though at times may lust for another's wife,
Or hold a grudge to prolong any strife.

And
Pharisees gave to each important cause,
And often to pray they would take a pause.
They'd fast so you'd see their anguish with ease,
While their motive never was God to please,
But for impressing folks while on their knees.

So,
Exceed righteousness of scribes as Christ taught,
Keep God's laws both in actions and in thought.
Beat righteousness of Pharisees this way,
Just give to needy while you fast and pray,
But don't seek glory and more praise each day.

Matthew 5:21-22

"You have heard that it was said to those of ancient times, 'You shall not murder'; and 'whoever murders shall be liable to judgment.' But I say to you that if you are angry with a brother or sister, you will be liable to judgment; and if you insult a brother or sister, you will be liable to the council; and if you say, 'You fool,' you will be liable to the hell of fire. [NRSV]

There's More to the
6th Commandment

Murder has always been considered a serious crime;
    How about making one feel he's not worth a dime?
Tearing people down may seem to elevate you higher;
    But It'll come back to haunt and set you on fire.

Venting your anger at someone may seem to you quite fine,
    But seriously then you are being quite blind.
Your anger will likely cause one to shake and to cower,
    And to feel as if dead lacking any power.

You can increase a person's misery with an insult,
    Causing him to think all the trouble is his fault.
And finally while you are calling him a worthless fool,
    You cause great depression, and that is truly cruel.

If you take a person's life, you eliminate his dreams;
    This obviously can be done by other schemes.
So regarding the 6th commandment there is a lot more:
    Kill one's spirit and he will be forever sore.

Matthew 5:23-26

So when you are offering your gift at the altar, if you remember that your brother or sister has something against you, leave your gift there before the altar and go; first be reconciled to your brother or sister, and then come and offer your gift. Come to terms quickly with your accuser while you are on the way to court with him, or your accuser may hand you over to the judge, and the judge to the guard, and you will be thrown into prison. Truly I tell you, you will never get out until you have paid the last penny.
[NRSV]

Order of Worship

First, avoid all litigation,
And seek reconciliation;
Then go to God with elation
To give a liberal donation.

Matthew 5:27-30

"You have heard that it was said, 'You shall not commit adultery.' But I say to you that everyone who looks at a woman with lust has already committed adultery with her in his heart. If your right eye causes you to sin, tear it out and throw it away; it is better for you to lose one of your members than for your whole body to be thrown into hell. And if your right hand causes you to sin cut it off and throw it away; it is better for you to lose one of your members than for your whole body to go into hell. [NRSV]

There's More to the 7th Commandment

Avoid adultery, God commanded;
Besides that, more is demanded.
To obey Jesus, it's a must
To never ever dwell on lust.

Thus, don't continue on this dwelling
As you sin and keep rebelling.
If you should lose an eye or hand,
That beats ignoring this command.

Matthew 5:31-32

"It was also said, 'Whoever divorces his wife, let him give her a certificate of divorce.' But I say to you that anyone who divorces his wife, except on the ground of unchastity, causes her to commit adultery; and whoever marries a divorced woman commits adultery. [NRSV]

(See also Mark 10:11-12, Luke 16:18)

The Innocent Sinner

During Christ's time men strutted with piety
In a male oriented society;
A man could do most anything with his life
So long as he'd leave alone another's wife;
On the other hand, a woman left marooned,
A damaged property this wife was assumed.
     Societal norms have become more sane;
     Thus, one is required to use one's brain.

16

But God always intended marriage for life;
So, what about divorcing a faithful wife?
If she should remarry, is that adultery?
How could one justify that at all to be?
When adultery for the couple is claimed,
The fact is that neither of them is to blame.
> Societal norms have become more sane;
> Thus, one is required to use one's brain.

Jesus did not bring change to society;
He just changed hearts without notoriety.
Societal norms then changed for the better,
Adjustments needed to keep to the letter;
So now one divorced whether woman or man,
A new faithful life he or she may command.
> Societal norms have become more sane;
> Thus, one is required to use one's brain.

What about a marriage that simply has died,
And the couple decides not together abide?
Which is guilty of sin I try to decide;
Then it's I for being judgmental with pride.
In divorces there clearly are no winners,
So don't accuse victims of being sinners.
> Societal norms have become more sane;
> Thus, one is required to use one's brain.

Matthew 5:33-37

"Again, you have heard that it was said to those of ancient times, 'You shall not swear falsely, but carry out the vows you have made to the Lord.' But I say to you, Do not swear at all, either by heaven, for it is the throne of God, or by the earth, for it is his footstool, or by Jerusalem, for it is the city of the great King. And do not swear by your head for you cannot make one hair white or black. Let your word be 'Yes, Yes' or 'No, No'; anything more than this comes from the evil one. [NRSV]

Integrity

Don't use God's name in what you say
In a careless or indifferent way,
Nor utter vulgar, gutter talk
As you go on your daily walk.

It's in bad taste, not commended;
Avoiding such is recommended;
But what did Christ likely convey?
The next verse will clearly portray.

Be honest, no need for an oath,
And deception is an act to loathe.
Complete honesty is a must
To be a person all will trust.

So make no pledge to any man;
Just agree to do the best you can.
You don't know what tomorrow brings;
So trust in God and to God cling.

Matthew 5:38-42

"You have heard that it was said, 'An eye for an eye and a tooth for a tooth.' But I say to you, Do not resist an evil doer. But if anyone strikes you on the right cheek, turn the other also; and if anyone wants to sue you and take your coat, give your cloak as well; and if anyone forces you to go one mile, go also the second mile. Give to everyone who begs from you, and do not refuse anyone who wants to borrow from you. [NRSV]

(See also Luke 6:29-30)

Neutralize a Conflict

If someone hits your face or arm,
　　Or greatly hurts your feelings,
You first would like to do him harm,
　　And then to leave him reeling.

To end the conflict is the best,
　　Although it seems like blindness;
Just put the thought of fight to rest,
　　And show your rival kindness.

Matthew 5:43-48

"You have heard that it was said, 'You shall love your neighbor and hate your enemy.' But I say to you, Love your enemies and pray for those who persecute you, so that you may be children of your Father in heaven; for he makes his sun rise on the evil and on the good, and sends rain on the righteous and on the unrighteous. For if you love those who love you, what reward do you have? Do not even the tax collectors do the same? And if you greet only your brothers and sisters, what more are you doing than others? Do not even the Gentiles do the same? Be perfect, therefore, as your heavenly Father is perfect. [NRSV]

(See also Luke 6:27-28, 32-36)

Love Your Enemy

Loving some people can be quite a pain,
Bin Laden, Hitler, or Saddam Hussein.
Perhaps one should start with a smaller load,
Showing kindness to all those on life's road.

Some may seem like an enemy to you
With all the mean things while driving they do.
But their situations, you do not know;
Thus, don't seek revenge; just let them go.

One's mom may be at a clinic dying;
He's rushing to be with her and crying.
Another may be late for an exam,
After staying up all night just to cram.

Loving those drivers is not hard to do,
If only you put yourself in their shoes.
So don't let your emotions drive the day;
Instead love others and for them just pray.

But must we love the depraved evil guy;
According to Jesus, we should, but why?
You can never trust him; he'll always lie,
And he enjoys causing others to cry.

Perhaps it's helpful to just take a look
At what else we find in God's Holy Book.
A good place to look—the Psalmists of old,
As they were talking with God and quite bold.

One hated with perfect hatred he said,*
And clearly wished all his enemies dead.
Another admitted he'd be quite thrilled,
For his foes' babies' heads bashed and blood spilled.**

God spoke to men through prophets in verses,
But words of the Psalmists were vice versa.
To God, the Psalmist did pour out his heart,
And that's a good thing, and it's always smart.

So be honest with God; give it a try,
And you'll approach loving all by and by.
Perfection's not possible in this life;
But seek compassion avoiding all strife.

---

*Psalms 139:22—I hate them with perfect hatred; I count them my
  enemies. [NRSV]

**Psalms 137:9—Happy shall they be who take your little ones and dash
  them against the rock! [NRSV]

Matthew 6:1-4

"Beware of practicing your piety before others in order to be seen by them; for then you have no reward from your Father in heaven.

"So whenever you give alms, do not sound a trumpet before you, as the hypocrites do in the synagogues and in the streets, so that they may be praised by others. Truly I tell you, they have received their reward. But when you give alms, do not let your left hand know what your right hand is doing, so that your alms may be done in secret; and your Father who sees in secret will reward you. [NRSV]

The Principle of Anonymity

You may meet poor folks on streets
Who don't have enough to eat;
Toward a life of crime some strive,
In order that their kids survive.

You may give much in your name,
So you'll get a lot of fame.
Folks will say, "What a great guy!
God will reward him in the sky."

But for true rewards from God,
When your body's under sod,
Give so only God would know,
From whom all this kindness flowed.

Matthew 6:5-8

"And whenever you pray, do not be like the hypocrites, for they love to stand and pray in the synagogues and at the street corners, so that they may be seen by others. Truly I tell you, they have received their reward. But whenever you pray, go into your room and shut the door and pray to your Father who is in secret; and your Father who sees in secret will reward you.

"When you are praying, do not heap up empty phrases as the Gentiles do; for they think that they will be heard because of their many words. Do not be like them, for your Father knows what you need before you ask him. [NRSV]

The Sincere Prayer

Public prayers are particularly powerful
In impressing, informing, and indoctrinating;
But, secrecy serves and satisfies our Savior; so,

When I pray, throughout the day,
Whether thanking or requesting, I
Will be silently conversing,
While this world is oblivious;
What I mean, I won't be obvious.

Matthew 6:9-15

"Pray then in this way:
> *Our Father in heaven,*
> *hallowed be your name.*
> *Your kingdom come.*
> *Your will be done, on earth as it is in heaven.*
> *Give us this day our daily bread.*
> *And forgive us our debts,*
>> *as we also have forgiven our debtors.*
> *And do not bring us to the time of trial,*
>> *but rescue us from the evil one.*

For if you forgive others their trespasses, your heavenly Father will also forgive you; but if you do not forgive others, neither will your Father forgive your trespasses. [NRSV]

(See also Luke 11:2-4)

Seeking Forgiveness

Complex prayers are not a must;
Just say where you put your trust;
And request your basic needs;
Ask God's help from sin and greed.

Ask forgiveness for your sins;
First forgive your fellow men.
This should not be so scary;
Peace with all adversaries.

Matthew 6:16-18

"And whenever you fast, do not look dismal like the hypocrites, for they disfigure their faces so as to show others that they are fasting. Truly I tell you, they have received their reward. But when you fast, put oil on your head and wash your face, so that your fasting may be seen not by others but by your Father who is in secret; and your Father who sees in secret will reward you. [NRSV]

Fasting

In some ancient societies,
Fasting was done as piety.
To them such acts would please their God;
Although to us that may seem odd.

You may search Scripture until blind,
But you would be hard-pressed to find,
How starving benefits mankind;
Regarding fasting, never mind.

But giving this a bit more thought,
Surrendering what could be bought,
Will free up cash to give the poor;
Then fasting is holy for sure.

If you fast to impress others,
Not aiding sisters or brothers,
Then God's the one you won't impress;
In fact, it's entirely worthless.

Matthew 6:19-24

"Do not store up for yourselves treasures on earth, where moth and rust consume and where thieves break in and steal; but store up for yourselves treasures in heaven, where neither moth nor rust consumes and where thieves do not break in and steal. For where your treasure is, there your heart will be also.

"The eye is the lamp of the body. So if your eye is healthy, your whole body will be full of light; but if your eye is unhealthy, your whole body will be full of darkness. If then the light in you is darkness, how great is the darkness!

"No one can serve two masters; for a slave will either hate the one and love the other or be devoted to the one and despise the other. You cannot serve God and wealth. [NRSV]

(See also Luke 12:33-34, 16:13)

The Divine Savings Plan

Your treasures on earth can lead to trouble:
    The stock market's subject to crash;
Real estate ventures can become rubble;
    Con artists may capture your cash.

Inflation can wipe your savings away;
    Lose all from a pointless lawsuit.
Your employment may not for long stay,
    For your boss may give you the boot.

Put treasures in heaven, and be secure,
    Though some say you're out of your mind;
You will know that you have nothing to fear;
    In Heav'n extra treasure you'll find.

Treasure in Heaven is easy for you;
    Find it rewarding and fun;
Giving much to the poor is what you do,
    Confirmed in Mark 10:21.

So what does treasure in Heaven imply?
    Christ suggests there is no guessing;
It's that those in Heaven, after they die,
    Won't all enjoy the same blessing.

A healthy eye gives your whole body light;
    A sick eye makes everything dark;
A relation with God makes your life bright;
    A sick relation has no spark.

If you think you can keep God number one,
    While hoarding money is your game,
Impossible! you'll be spiritually done;
    Serving two masters is to blame.

Matthew 6:25-34

"Therefore I tell you, do not worry about your life, what you will eat or what you will drink, or about your body, what you will wear. Is not life more than food, and the body more than clothing? Look at the birds of the air; they neither sow nor reap nor gather into barns, and yet your heavenly Father feeds them. Are you not of more value than they? And can any of you by worrying add a single hour to your span of life? And why do you worry about clothing? Consider the lilies of the field, how they grow; they neither toil nor spin, yet I tell you even Solomon in all his glory was not clothed like one of these. But if God so clothes the grass of the field, which is alive today and tomorrow is thrown into the oven, will he not much more clothe you—you of little faith? Therefore do not worry, saying 'What will we eat?' or 'What will we drink?' or 'What will we wear?' For it is the Gentiles who strive for all these things; and indeed your heavenly Father knows that you need all these things. But strive first for the kingdom of God and his righteousness, and all these things will be given to you as well.

"So do not worry about tomorrow, for tomorrow will bring worries of its own. Today's trouble is enough for today. [NRSV]

(See also Luke 12:22-31)

Anxiety

If you have control, then worrying is absurd.
How about considering the flight of the birds?
Before freezing or starving God helps them time it,
So they migrate to a favorable climate.
If God knows the birds and gives them guidance in flight,
Then you can bet God will help you do what is right.

There are situations where you have no control;
Then avoiding all anguish should be your main goal.
Now consider the lilies how great they're arrayed;
They take what they get neither worry nor afraid.
God so cares for lilies that are gone tomorrow;
You're much better; no need for anguish or sorrow.

Therefore, don't be anxious when wealth you would keep;
Instead, just trust God, and God's Kingdom go seek.
And it may surprise you as your needs come to you,
When Seeking God's wisdom in all that you do.
So keep focused on present while doing what's right,
Expecting with God's help, a tomorrow that's bright.

Matthew 7:1-5

"Do not judge, so that you may not be judged. For with the judgment you make you will be judged, and the measure you give will be the measure you get. Why do you see the speck in your neighbor's eye, but do not notice the log in your own eye? Or how can you say to your neighbor, 'Let me take the speck out of your eye,' while the log is in your own eye? You hypocrite, first take the log out of your own eye, and then you will see clearly to take the speck out of your neighbor's eye. [NRSV]

(See also Luke 6:37, 41-42)

The Judgmental Attitude

It's easy to criticize or condemn,
Because in others I can see their sin;
That is because the same sin is within.

Before attempting to correct someone,
I must first correct the stuff I have done.
Clearly, it is best from judging to run.

So then for God to overlook my fault,
I must be careful never to insult,
And bring my judging others to a halt.

Matthew 7:6

"Do not give what is holy to dogs; and do not throw your pearls before swine, or they will trample them under foot and turn and maul you. [NRSV]

Holy Pearls

Don't give what's holy to the dogs,
Nor cast your pearls to the hogs.
In God's word you may discover,
When searching cover to cover,
A pearl that is a real treasure
Since it gives you lots of pleasure.

Sharing it may bring a blessing;
Others may just leave you guessing.
Some will welcome what you share,
While some fanatics best to spare.
They may kick and toss it around,
Trampling it into the ground.

Matthew 7:7-11

"Ask and it will be given you; search, and you will find; knock, and the door will be opened for you. For everyone who asks receives, and everyone who searches finds, and for everyone who knocks, the door will be opened. Is there anyone among you who, if your child asks for bread, will give a stone? Or if the child asks for a fish, will give a snake? If you then, who are evil, know how to give good gifts to your children, how much more will your Father in heaven give good things to those who ask him! [NRSV]

(See also Luke 11:9-13)

Ask and You Will Receive

Ask and you'll receive; I doubt it and here's why:
When you pray for healing, a friend may still die;
The answer's not certain regardless how you try.

When you ask, you may not get what you request.
Maybe that's because God always knows what's best;
Or could it be that God's putting you to the test?

Though what you ask of God you may not receive,
You may get something that you could not conceive;
It may be peace of mind, as anguish takes a leave.

Matthew 7:12

"In everything do to others as you would have them do to you; for this is the law and the prophets. [NRSV]

(See also Luke 6:31)

The Golden Rule

The Old Testament's full of truth; some of it seems cruel;
To comprehend it scholars spend many years in school.
But never let that frustrate you, and don't be a fool,
For Jesus summarized it all with the Golden Rule.

Matthew 7:13-14

"Enter through the narrow gate; for the gate is wide and the road is easy that leads to destruction, and there are many who take it. For the gate is narrow and the road is hard that leads to life, and there are few who find it. [NRSV]

(See also Luke 13:23-24)

Choose the Road Less Taken

Although all Jesus spoke is true,
Some of the things are hard to do;
Most people will not even try,
With all His teachings to comply;
The path of most women and men,
Ends up in destruction and sin.

So take a direction askew,
All things in your life will be new;
Putting your confidence in Him,
Life in God's kingdom will begin.
You've made a great choice for your way;
Blessings are yours—come what may.

Matthew 7:15-23

"Beware of false prophets, who come to you in sheep's clothing but inwardly are ravenous wolves. You will know them by their fruits. Are grapes gathered from thorns, or figs from thistles? In the same way, every good tree bears good fruit, but the bad tree bears bad fruit. A good tree cannot bear bad fruit, nor can a bad tree bear good fruit. Every tree that does not bear good fruit is cut down and thrown into the fire. Thus you will know them by their fruits.

"Not everyone who says to me, "Lord, Lord," will enter the kingdom of heaven, but only the one who does the will of my Father in heaven. On that day many will say to me, "Lord, Lord, did we not prophesy in your name and cast out demons in your name, and do many deeds of power in your name?" Then I will declare to them, "I never knew you; go away from me, you evildoers. [NRSV]

False Prophets

Some are speaking for God they claim,
    Though not at all sincere;
They are truly playing a game,
    And you should run in fear.

Such false prophets are affective,
    And convincing they seem,
Though their actions are defective
    In presenting false schemes.

Oh that guy from Indiana,
    A following he swayed;
They ended up in Guyana,
    Swallowing laced Kool-aid.

An astute follower should've seen
    Marriages disrupted;
His teachings were false and obscene,
    His demands corrupted.

They should have seen things getting worse,
    Abiding by his side,
While they're being taught to rehearse
    Committing suicide.

The Waco guy in retrospect,
    Corrupt as he could be;
His followers seemed to neglect
    To think through and to flee.

His group may have been quite lazy;
    All children he would sire.
Revelation teachings crazy,
    They ended up in fire.

Look at the California guy,
    Makes you want to vomit!
Soon he and his followers died,
    Thought they'd join a comet.

It's important to remember,
    Though many say "Lord, Lord!"
Of God's group they're not a member;
    So run! There's no reward.

Matthew 7:24-27

"Everyone then who hears these words of mine and acts on them will be like a wise man who built his house on rock. The rain fell, the floods came, and the winds blew and beat on that house, but it did not fall because it had been founded on rock. And everyone who hears these words of mine and does not act on them will be like a foolish man who built his house on sand. The rain fell, and the floods came, and the winds blew and beat against that house, and it fell—and great was its fall! [NRSV]

(See also Luke 6:47-49)

A Firm Foundation

Most lives are like a house built on a beach,
    With a foundation of nothing but sand;
Longevity for the house's out of reach;
    Likewise, the legacies of most are bland.

So build your life on a firm foundation;
    That's living by the *Sermon on the Mount*;
Present and future extrapolation,
    Inspiring legacy will be found.

But without having this firm foundation,
    When the turbulent storms of life erupt,
Your hopes, aspirations, and vocation,
    Can all be destroyed or become corrupt.

In God's Kingdom with foundation that's firm,
    You can't avoid storms wherever they're from;
But you'll weather them regardless how stern.
    Therefore, focused and stronger you'll become.

Then you will know life is on the right trend,
    With all things being so gratifying;
For being in God's Kingdom will not end;
    Life continues even after dying.

Chapter 2

The Sermon on the Plain

Joy and Woe

Joy and woe are woven fine,
A clothing for the soul divine,
Under every grief and pine,
Runs a joy with silken twine.

It is right, it should be so;
Man was made for joy and woe.
And when this we rightly know,
Thro' the world we safely go.

-William Blake

Introduction to Luke's Beatitudes

We have the *Sermon on the Mount*,
  And *Sermon on the Plain*;
In both beatitudes are found,
  But they are not the same.

On the plain, disciples learned,
  Not only are some blessed;
But also others may be burned,
  At least put to the test.

Joy and Woe, by William Blake,
  Tells a similar theme;
The one seeming to take the cake,
  Finds a horrible scene.

Both good and bad beatitudes
  Are part of Luke's story;
The haves may end in servitude,
  Have-nots receive glory.

Luke 6:17-26

He came down with them and stood on a level place, with a great crowd of his disciples and a great multitude of people from all Judea, Jerusalem, and the coast of Tyre and Sidon. They had come to hear him and to be healed of their diseases; and those who were troubled with unclean spirits were cured. And all in the crowd were trying to touch him, for power came out from him and healed all of them.

Then he looked up at his disciples and said:

"Blessed are you who are poor,

for yours is the kingdom of God.

"Blessed are you who are hungry now,

for you will be filled.

"Blessed are you who weep now,

for you will laugh.

"Blessed are you when people hate you, and when they exclude you, revile you, and defame you on account of the Son of Man. Rejoice in that day and leap for joy, for surely your reward is great in heaven; for that is what their ancestors did to the prophets.

"But woe to you who are rich,

for you have received your consolation.

"Woe to you who are full now,

for you will be hungry.

"Woe to you who are laughing now,

for you will mourn and weep.

"Woe to you when all speak well of you, for that is what their ancestors did to the false prophets. [NRSV]

Blessings and Woes

You are blessed if poor, hungry, or sad;
You'll be in God's kingdom, filled, and glad.
And you're blessed when your treatment is bad;
Your situation's a passing fad.

Predecessors were treated that way,
And some with their lives, they had to pay.
They've left great legacies for today;
Jesus', Bonhoeffer's, and King's lives stay.

Woe to you rich, full, in happy state;
Things will reverse at a rapid rate.
Some may be speaking of you as great;
Such people, history has learned to hate.

Christ's sayings were understood by Blake,
Where joy and woe bring pleasure and ache.
In your life you have too much at stake,
To let your troubles cause you to break.

Luke 6:27-36

"But I say to you that listen, Love your enemies, do good to those who hate you, bless those who curse you, pray for those who abuse you. If someone strikes you on the cheek, offer the other also; and from anyone who takes away your coat do not withhold even your shirt. Give to everyone who begs from you; and if anyone takes away your goods, do not ask for them again. Do to others as you would have them do to you.

"If you love those who love you, what credit is that to you? For even sinners love those who love them. If you do good to those who do good to you, what credit is that to you? For even sinners do the same. If you lend to those from whom you hope to receive, what credit is that to you? Even sinners lend to sinners, to receive as much again. But love your enemies, do good, and lend, expecting nothing in return. Your reward will be great, and you will be children of the Most High; for he is kind to the ungrateful and wicked. Be merciful, just as your Father is merciful. [NRSV]

(See also Matthew 5:39-48)

Show Loving Kindness
to Adversaries

To your foe show loving kindness,
　　Although he curses you.
Work with him to relieve all stress;
　　Pray for the abuser too.

If he should break right through your door,
　　And take some of your stuff,
Consider giving him some more,
　　So he will have enough.

If from him, you receive a strike,
　　Don't think of fighting back;
Nor should you run or take a hike;
　　Permit another whack.

If to friends only, you show love,
　　What will that do for you?
There'll be no credit from above;
　　Sinners act that way too.

So to your enemy show love;
　　It's gracious you will find.
As God shows mercy from above,
　　Be merciful and kind.

Luke 6:37-38

"Do not judge, and you will not be judged; do not condemn, and you will not be condemned. Forgive, and you will be forgiven; give, and it will be given to you. A good measure, pressed down, shaken together, running over, will be put into your lap; for the measure you give will be the measure you get back." [NRSV]

The Law of Reciprocity

To avoid judgment do not judge;
To be forgiv'n don't hold a grudge;
To get blessings without measure,
Giving much will be your pleasure.

Luke 6:39-42

He also told them a parable: "Can a blind person guide a blind person? Will not both fall into a pit? A disciple is not above the teacher, but everyone who is fully qualified will be like the teacher. Why do you see the speck in your neighbor's eye, but do not notice the log in your own eye? Or how can you say to your neighbor, 'Friend, let me take out the speck in your eye,' when you yourself do not see the log in your own eye? You hypocrite, first take the log out of your own eye, and then you will see clearly to take the speck out of your neighbor's eye. [NRSV]

Clean Up Your Own Act

An unqualified leader,
With his followers will fall;
An unqualified teacher,
And his students will all stall;
Each must clean up his own act,
To help his neighbor get on track.

Luke 6:43-45

"No good tree bears bad fruit, nor again does a bad tree bear good fruit. For each tree is known by its own fruit. Figs are not gathered from thorns, nor are grapes picked from a bramble bush. The good person out of the good treasure of the heart, produces good, and the evil person out of evil treasure produces evil; for it is out of the abundance of the heart that the mouth speaks. [NRSV]

The Truly Good Person

A tree producing good fruit is good,
Behaving in the way it should.
A person acting as Christ suggests,
Is one who really is the best.
If it's righteous people that you seek,
Pay attention to how they speak.

A tree producing bad fruit is bad;
It's a worthless tree, oh how sad.
A person ignoring what Christ said,
Is one who is spiritually dead.
One speaking with anger or deceit,
Can't be trusted he'll likely cheat.

Luke 6:46-49

"Why do you call me 'Lord, Lord,' and do not do what I tell you? I will show you what someone is like who comes to me, hears my words, and acts on them. That one is like a man building a house, who dug deeply and laid the foundation on rock; when a flood arose, the river burst against that house but could not shake it, because it had been well built. But the one who hears and does not act is like a man who built a house on the ground without a foundation. When the river burst against it, immediately it fell, and great was the ruin of that house." [NRSV]

(See also Matthew 7:24-27)

Note: The following poem is composed of three Haiku style verses.

Foundational Teaching

A good foundation,
A secure habitation,
Survive a harsh storm.

A bad foundation,
It's an unsafe location,
A disaster's born.

It's metaphoric;
Christ's teachings are euphoric,
Safety from life's storms.

Chapter 3

Misc. Sayings

Luke 4:18-21

"The Spirit of the Lord is upon me,
because he has anointed me
to bring good news to the poor.
He has sent me to proclaim release to the captives
and recovery of sight to the blind,
to let the oppressed go free,
to proclaim the year of the Lord's favor."
*And he rolled up the scroll, gave it again to the attendant, and sat down. The eyes of all in the synagogue were fixed on him. Then he began to say to them, "***Today this scripture has been fulfilled in your hearing.*** [NRSV]*

Jesus' Mission

Jesus was anointed from above,
To bring to the poor good news and love;
Blind people were made able to see;
The captives and oppressed were set free.

The year of the Lord's favor was preached;
That is, God's kingdom put within reach.
This was predicted by Isaiah; *
Yet, as to Christ, they had no idea.

*Isaiah 61:1, 2b—The spirit of the Lord GOD is upon me,
          because the LORD has anointed me;
          he has sent me to bring good news to the oppressed,
          to bind up the brokenhearted,
          to proclaim liberty to the captives,
          and release to the prisoners;
          to proclaim the year of the LORD's favor, [NRSV]

Matthew 10:5-6

These twelve Jesus sent out with the following instructions: **Go nowhere among the Gentiles, and enter no town of the Samaritans, but go rather to the lost sheep of the house of Israel.** [NRSV]

Matthew 15:21-28

Jesus left that place and went away to the district of Tyre and Sidon. Just then a Canaanite woman from that region came out and started shouting, "Have mercy on me, Lord, Son of David; my daughter is tormented by a demon." But he did not answer her at all. And his disciples came and urged him saying, "Send her away, for she keeps shouting after us." He answered, **"I was sent only to the lost sheep of the house of Israel."** *But she came and knelt before him, saying, "Lord, help me." He answered,* **"It is not fair to take the children's food and throw it to the dogs."** *She said, Yes, Lord, yet even the dogs eat the crumbs that fall from their masters' table." Then Jesus answered her,* **"Woman, great is your faith! Let it be done for you as you wish."** *And her daughter was healed instantly.* [NRSV]

(See also Mark 7:24-30)

Was Jesus Aware?

Jesus gave His disciples their mission:
Go to the Jews with complete permission.
Regarding Gentiles—total omission.

Was Jesus aware of why He was here?
Was going to Gentiles something to fear?
Or was His mission totally unclear?

Consider next the woman from Canaan,
Whose daughter was possessed by a demon;
To cure her daughter, Jesus was the one.

Because she was foreign Jesus refused;
She continued to ignore the excuse.
Then He insulted her; seems like abuse.

But to her Jesus finally complied,
When she cleverly and humbly replied.
What an example! She swallowed all pride.

Was He surprised when He finally did find,
He was the Savior of all humankind?
But wouldn't He have known since He is divine?

Could there be more because this is unclear?
Was He then testing this woman right here?
Regarding these questions I'll just steer clear.

Luke 5:36-39

He also told them a parable; **"No one tears a piece from a new garment and sews it on an old garment; otherwise the new will be torn, and the piece from the new will not match the old. And no one puts new wine into old wineskins; otherwise the new wine will burst the skins, and will be spilled, and the skins will be destroyed. But new wine must be put into fresh wineskins. And no one after drinking old wine desires new wine, but says, 'The old is good.'"** [NRSV]

(See also Matthew 9:16-17, Mark 2:23-22)

Timeless
Scriptures

Scriptures are timeless,
But avoid being mindless;
You must use your brain.

New situations,
Ancient interpretations,
Can't be used the same.

Matthew 8:20

And Jesus said to him, **"Foxes have holes, and birds of the air have nests; but the Son of Man has nowhere to lay his head."** [NRSV]

(See also Luke 9:58)

Matthew 11:29-30

Take my yoke upon you, and learn from me; for I am gentle and humble in heart, and you will find rest for your souls. For my yoke is easy, and my burden is light." [NRSV]

Matthew 8:22

But Jesus said to him, **"Follow me, and let the dead bury their own dead.** [NRSV]

(See also Luke 9:60)

Matthew 11:28

"Come to me, all you that are weary and are carrying heavy burdens, and I will give you rest. [NRSV]

The Hard Commitment Proves Easy

Following Jesus may seem hard;
Some conveniences may be barred.
But learn from Him, and you will find,
His burden's light; He's meek and kind.

Leave behind things with no meaning;
A new life will be your leaning.
So come to Jesus; be his guest;
If you're weary, He'll give you rest.

Mark 2:27-28

Then he said to them, **"The Sabbath was made for man, not man for the Sabbath; so the Son of Man is Lord even of the Sabbath."**
[NIV]

The Sabbath is for Our Benefit

Must we not work one day in seven?
That's a law that came from heaven.
It was not meant to cause you grief;
Instead was meant to bring relief.

So if your work is overwhelming,
Causing frustration and ailing,
Go on and do what you think best;
Then you'll receive your needed rest.

Some pious ones may say you're sinning,
But their faith is just beginning.
If you don't abuse Commandment 4,
Consider their words; then ignore.

Mark 7:15

there is nothing from outside a person that by going in can defile, but the things that come out are what defile." [NRSV]

(See also Matthew 15:11)

Defilement via the Mouth
(uni- or bi-directional?)

Is it not what goes in that defiles man?
It seems alcoholic beverages can;
They'll occasionally make one act crazy,
And may make him forgetful or lazy.

So much gluttony, is it a pity?
An epidemic of obesity;
One's body certainly won't be the same,
When he's playing the over-eating game.

Can't food exposed to certain bacteria
Result in dreadful sickness criteria?
Perhaps one with knowledge needs to explain,
Why only the output we should refrain.

But if it's His meaning you want to find,
Then this must be what Jesus had in mind:
Effects of a bad meal soon will be past,
But fallout from words forever will last.

Matthew 9:11-13

*When the Pharisees saw this, they said to his disciples, "Why does your teacher eat with tax collectors and sinners?" But when he heard this, he said, **"Those who are well have no need of a physician, but those who are sick. Go and learn what this means, 'I desire mercy, not sacrifice.' For I have come to call not the righteous, but sinners.** [NRSV]*

Reach out to Sinners

Jesus came for the needy and blind,
    Whether spiritual or physical;
At times it's needful to cross the line,
    With traditions that seem biblical.

To please God it's good to remember,
    Compared to traditions, Mercy's best;
Whether it is June or December,
    Reach out to sinners and you'll be blest.

Matthew 11:2-6

When John heard in prison what the Messiah was doing, he sent word by his disciples and said to him, "Are you the one who is to come, or are we to wait for another?" **Jesus answered them, "Go and tell John what you hear and see: the blind receive their sight, the lame walk, the lepers are cleansed, the deaf hear, the dead are raised, and the poor have good news brought to them. And blessed is anyone who takes no offense at me."** [NRSV]

(See also Luke 7:19-23)

Was Jesus the Christ?

They thought the Christ would restore their Kingdom;
    John was beginning to doubt.
"Is Jesus the one expected to come?
    What is it all about?"

So John sent messengers to enquire,
    "Jesus, could you be the one?"
Since for John to know, it seemed quite dire,
    So he could call it done.

Jesus only evaded the question,
    Refused to answer straight;
And only hinted at a suggestion,
    Knowing they'd take the bait.

Why did He evade what was asked by John,
    Stating what John knew was so?
He was not trying to trick or to con;
    Then why not a yes or no?

"Behold, the lame are made able to walk,
    And the blind receive their sight.
The deaf are made able to hear and talk;
    For the poor, the news is bright."

"The lepers are cleansed," is what He said;
    "Just trust in what you see.
Some that were dead did not stay dead;
    Take no offense in me."

Though the things Jesus said and did were good,
    That's not what was expected;
Israel's kingdom wasn't coming as should;
    As Christ He'd be rejected.

To receive glory, Jesus resisted,
    And things went on the same.
So the mystery of Christ still persisted,
    'Til Christ became His name.

Matthew 13:57

And they took offense at him. But Jesus said to them, **"Prophets are not without honor, except in their own country and in their own house."** [NRSV]

(See also Mark 6:4, Luke 4:24)

The Unsung Hero

One may find a spiritual gift
   She never knew she had.
Proclaiming it may cause a rift
   As locals think she's bad.

If she moves far enough from home,
   Where folks don't know her past,
At first she may seem all alone,
   But here hope may be vast.

Her new talent or idea,
   She hadn't advanced before,
Won't be looked at as trivia;
   Folks will want to explore.

Luke 12:10

And everyone who speaks a word against the Son of Man will be forgiven; but whoever blasphemes against the Holy Spirit will not be forgiven. [NRSV]

(See also Matthew 12:32, Mark 3:28-29)

The Unpardonable Sin

A theme in Scripture from beginning to end,
Is that God willingly forgives any sin;
Now it appears God will at best come near it,
Not forgiving sin against Holy Spirit.

This biblical verse has caused anguish and scare;
Some wonder if they have committed this error.
Jesus meant to bring comfort—never distress;
So what this passage means is anyone's guess.

Luke 12:51

Do you think that I have come to bring peace to the earth? No, I tell you, but rather division! From now on five in one household will be divided, three against two and two against three; they will be divided:

> *Father against son*
> > *and son against father,*
>
> *Mother against daughter*
> > *And daughter against mother,*
>
> *Mother-in-law against her daughter-in-law*
> > *And daughter-in-law against*
> > > *Mother-in-law."*

[NRSV]

(See also Matthew 10:34-36)

The Prince of Peace
Brings Conflict

There are other examples we could present,
Who were famous for peace, but some did resent.
The peace-prize laureate Martin Luther King,
Preaching and acting his non-violent thing,
Within all of the Christian community,
There clearly wasn't what we'd call unity.

So how can the Prince of Peace bring divisions?
It may be due to alternate decisions;
As one trusts Christ and becomes a follower,
The others keep trying not to allow her.
Then she tries donating their silver and gold,
But her spouse demands they continue to hold.

With one-dimensional political sphere,
Party alignment makes one's views all so clear.
With fellow church members this can cause conflicts,
As some church ethos align with politics.
So to follow Jesus it may require,
Many conflicts that at times are quite dire.

Mark 4:30-32

He also said, "With what can we compare the kingdom of God, or what parable will we use for it? It is like a mustard seed, which, when sown upon the ground, is the smallest of all the seeds on earth; yet when it is sown it grows up and becomes the greatest of all shrubs, and puts forth large branches, so that the birds of the air can make nests in its shade." [NRSV]

(See also Matthew 13:31-32, Luke 13:18-19)

Luke 17:20-21

Once Jesus was asked by the Pharisees when the kingdom of God was coming, and he answered, "The kingdom of God is not coming with things that can be observed; nor will they say, 'Look, here it is!' or 'There it is!' For, in fact, the kingdom of God is among you." [NRSV]

The Expanding Kingdom

From the time one is born through the age of two,
God's kingdom is only for him through and through;
And it's obvious to him, and it's a fact
For him alone, all people and things do act.

Even the sun, the moon, and all of the stars,
Always follow him when traveling in cars.
As he gets older this kingdom gets bigger;
Now his whole family he'll also consider.

Then he discovers it's easy to remember,
Also belongs any fellow church member.
Later this kingdom expands its relations,
Includes all protestant denominations.

Then he learns of Catholics he didn't expect,
They don't worship Mary, just show great respect,
And they too are part of God's kingdom he finds;
It now has expanded much so don't be blind.

The next expansion needs a faith that's mature,
To see other creeds in God's kingdom for sure.
So God's kingdom among you once it begins,
It expands and expands with seeming no end.

Matthew 13:33

He told them another parable: **"The kingdom of heaven is like yeast that a woman took and mixed in with three measures of flour until all of it was leavened."** [NRSV]

(See also Luke 13:20-21)

Note: The following Haiku style verses summarize the previous poem.

Summary of the Expanding Kingdom

Kingdom of Heaven,
Is like bread full of leaven;
Small but will expand.

First all about me,
Then others are in I see;
Inclusive and grand.

Luke 14: 26

"Whoever comes to me and does not hate father and mother, wife and children, brothers and sisters, yes even life itself, cannot be my disciple. [NRSV]

Where Are the Family Values?

Should I despise my own wife and child?
    Must I then wish them all harm?
Could not Christ have said something more mild,
    And not brought such an alarm?

This verse found in Luke does seem quite clear;
    Yet I clearly reject it.
There must be another meaning here,
    So that I can accept it.

Perhaps Matthew's version,* which makes sense,
    Is closer to what Christ said;
Here He asks relative allegiance,
    And that leaves nothing to dread.

*Matthew 10:37-38—**Whoever loves father or mother more than me is not worthy of me; and whoever loves son or daughter more than me is not worthy of me; and whoever does not take up the cross and follow me is not worthy of me.** [NRSV]

Luke 18:18-23

A Certain ruler asked him, "Good Teacher, what must I do to inherit eternal life?" Jesus said to him, **"Why do you call me good? No one is good but God alone. You know the commandments: 'You shall not commit adultery; You shall not murder; You shall not steal; You shall not bear false witness; Honor your father and mother.'"** He replied, "I have kept all these since my youth." When Jesus heard this, he said to him, **"There is still one thing lacking. Sell all that you own and distribute the money to the poor, and you will have treasure in heaven; then come, follow me."** But when he heard this, he became sad; for he was very rich. [NRSV]

(See also Matthew 19:16-22, Mark 10:17-22)

Failing the Prerequisite Test

A rich man came to Jesus full of strife,
Asked what would keep him from eternal life;
Obeying commandments was his claim,
So Christ suggested a different blame.

"Sell your possessions is step number one,
And give all to those with little or none."
But such a plan did not bring him delight;
Surrendering wealth to him was a fright.

"Step two after giving up all of your stuff,
Is to follow Me; that's not so tough."
It seems that he did not get to step two;
Surrendering wealth was too much to do.

Luke 18:24-25

Jesus looked at him and said, **"How hard it is for those who have wealth to enter the kingdom of God! Indeed, it is easier for a camel to go through the eye of a needle than for someone who is rich to enter the kingdom of God."** [NRSV]

(See also Matthew 19:23-24, Mark 10:23-25)

Can a Rich Man Enter the Kingdom of Heaven?

Is salvation impossible if you're rich?
I can believe it; I don't fall in that niche;
Regardless of wealth that I'm able to store,
A rich person's one with a little bit more.

If I have two coats, I should give one away.*
Since I have several, what should I say?
By biblical standards, I'm rich as can be;
Now His philosophy is so hard to see.

*Luke 3:11

Matthew 18.21-22

Then Peter came to Jesus and asked, "Lord, how many times shall I forgive my brother when he sins against me? Up to seven times?" Jesus answered, **"I tell you, not seven times, but seventy-seven times."** [NIV]

Then came Peter to him and said, Lord, how oft shall my brother sin against me, and I forgive him? Till seven times? Jesus saith unto him, **I say not unto thee, Until seven times; but, Until seventy times seven.** [KJV]

Is There a Limit
to Forgiveness?

Peter suggested the limit of seven,
But Jesus put it at seventy-seven;
Some versions say it's seventy times seven,
    And that is four hundred and ninety.

Clearly it's not once or twice or seven times,
But you forgive a transgressor many times;
Symbolic numbers may be spoken at times,
    When the value is infinity.

Matthew 19:8

He said to them, "It was because you were so hard-hearted that Moses allowed you to divorce your wives, but from the beginning it was not so. [NRSV]

Not All Moses Said
is from God

Moses gave us laws by the score;
Some seem good, others we ignore.
Some biblical laws that seem odd
Were not handed down from our God.

Mark 12:16-17

And they brought it. And he saith unto them, **Whose is this image and superscription?** *And they said unto him, Caesar's. And Jesus answering said unto them,* **Render to Caesar the things that are Caesar's, and to God the things that are God's.** *And they marvelled at him.* [KJV]

(See also Matthew 22:19-22, Luke 20:23-26)

Beyond Money:
Donating Time & Talent

"Caesar's" image is on your currency;
Much must be rendered to his agency;
Therefore, you must never ever be lax,
When it comes to paying your income tax.

Likewise, you're created in God's image;
Thus, serving God is more than scrimmage.
Taxes require much money from you;
So to God, how much of yourself is due?

Mark 12:41-44

He sat down opposite the treasury, and watched the crowd putting money into the treasury. Many rich people put in large sums. A poor widow came and put in two small copper coins, which are worth a penny. Then he called his disciples and said to them, **"Truly I tell you, this poor widow has put in more than all those who are contributing to the treasury. For all of them have contributed out of their abundance; but she out of her poverty has put in everything she had, all she had to live on."** [NRSV]

(See also Luke 21:1-4)

Beyond Ten Percent:
The Graduated Tithe

A widow, who came from the slum,
Donated a small, paltry sum;
A rich man, with his donation,
Viewed the widow as vexation.

To God the widow gave much more,
As the man still kept much in store;
To God it's not your offered heap,
But it's how small the stash you keep.

Matthew 16:28

"Truly I tell you, there are some standing here who will not taste death before they see the Son of Man coming in his kingdom."
[NRSV]

Son of Man Coming in His Kingdom

While many were listening, Jesus said,
That He would return before they're all dead;
Obviously, by now, they have all died,
And we dread assuming that Jesus lied.

Is He not the same as the Son of Man?
Or did He describe some very strange plan?
Perhaps He came with Kingdom of Heaven,
In what follows Matthew 27.

That's where He came out of the grave alive,
Encouraging all for God's Kingdom to strive.
Does this fulfill it? Most can't accept it;
So we'll find something else to reflect it.

"Christians are the Body of Christ," said Paul;*
So the birth of the Church explains it all.
For 'Son of Man,' 'Church' is poor alias;
This interpretation is somewhat dubious.

Maybe He meant the day of Pentecost,
With the Holy Ghost coming to save the lost,
Meaning Jesus and Holy Ghost are the same;
This may not match the theological game.

Even for us with the Trinity creed,
He's not only God but a human breed;
Holy Ghost is God in Spiritual form—
Let's avoid a theological storm.

Another way to reconcile of course,
Is to assume Mark's Gospel was the source;
In Mark's verse "Son of Man" is omitted,**
A Pentecost answer is permitted.

*1 Corinthians 12:27—Now you are the body of Christ and individually members of it. [NRSV]

Mark 9:1—And he said to them, "Truly I tell you, there are some standing here, who will not taste death until they see that the kingdom of God has come with power.**" [NRSV] (See also Luke 9:27)

Matthew 25:31-46

"When the Son of man comes in his glory, and all the angels with him, he will sit on his throne in heavenly glory. All the nations will be gathered before him, and he will separate the people one from another as a shepherd separates the sheep from the goats. He will put the sheep on his right and the goats on his left.

"Then the King will say to those on his right, 'Come, you who are blessed by my Father; take your inheritance, the kingdom prepared for you since the creation of the world. For I was hungry, and you gave me something to eat, I was thirsty, and you gave me something to drink, I was a stranger, and you invited me in, I needed clothes and you clothed me: I was sick and you looked after me, I was in prison, and you came to visit me.

"Then the righteous will answer him, 'Lord, when did we see you hungry and feed you, or thirsty and give you something to drink? When did we see you a stranger and invite you in, or needing clothes and clothe you? When did we see you sick or in prison and go to visit you?

"The King will reply, 'I tell you the truth, whatever you did for one of the least of these brothers of mine, you did for me.'

"Then he will say to those on his left, 'Depart from me, you who are cursed, into the eternal fire prepared for the devil and his angels. For I was hungry and you gave me nothing to eat. I was thirsty and you gave me nothing to drink. I was a stranger and you did not invite me in. I needed clothes and you did not clothe me, I was sick and in prison and you did not look after me.'

"They also will answer, 'Lord, when did we see you hungry or thirsty or a stranger or needing clothes or sick or in prison, and did not help you?'

"He will reply, 'I tell you the truth, whatever you did not do for one of the least of these, you did not do for me.'

"Then they will go away to eternal punishment, but the righteous to eternal life." [NIV]

The Surprising Final Judgment

The last judgment will result in surprise;
The most selfless ones to the top will rise.
When told of all acts for Jesus they'd done,
They'll be surprised not remembering one;
It's because of all those needy and forlorn,
For whom acts of kindness they did perform.

But many who are full of piety,
And did little for the least in society,
Will be shocked when learning what they had done,
Because it was Jesus whom they had shunned.
They thought they needed no apology,
Counting on atonement theology.

Matthew 28:16-20

Now the eleven disciples went to Galilee, to the mountain to which Jesus had directed them. When they saw him, they worshiped him; but some doubted. And Jesus came and said to them, **"All authority in heaven and on earth has been given to me. Go therefore and make disciples of all nations, baptizing them in the name of the Father and of the Son and of the Holy Spirit, and teaching them to obey everything that I have commanded you. And remember, I am with you always, to the end of the age."** [NRSV]

The Great Commission

Just prior to Jesus' Ascension,
   After He had been declared dead,
Jesus gave us the Great Commission,
   All His teachings we are to spread;
It could be called the great omission,
   As we scorn the main things He said.

We're taught theology without end,
   With scant reference to His word;
Following the latest worldly trend,
   Counting much of His spiel absurd;
But to really keep Jesus our friend,
   We must stop following the herd.

So to obey Jesus all the way,
   And let Him and His teachings in,
Start heeding what we do and say,
   And practice love, avoiding sin;
Read the *Sermon on the Mount* today,
   And that's a good place to begin.

Biblical Index

63186782R00072

Made in the USA
Charleston, SC
30 October 2016